PAUL JACKSON

PAPIER MÂCHÉ

Illustrations: Terry Burton

Lions
An Imprint of HarperCollinsPublishers

introduction

Papier mâché means 'mashed paper' in French. It is a technique using layers of paper soaked in glue to make amazingly strong objects.

The Chinese were the first people to develop the technique of papier mâché. About two thousand years ago they discovered that it could be used to make strong body armour and helmets.

Later, in Europe, the technique supported a large industry making furniture, boxes, trays and many other things. But its uses don't stop at relatively small items. It has been used to make the walls and doors of all the houses in an entire Australian village, and even a complete papier mâché church in Norway!

Today, craftspeople throughout the world make and sell papier mâché bowls and jewellery, and artists use the technique to create all kinds of sculpture.

This book shows you how to make some simple but exciting projects such as bowls, boxes, hats and heads, and suggests ways to decorate them.

A section at the end of the book gives lots of ideas for further papier mâché projects and presents. However, once you have mastered the basics outlined in this book, you will be able to use papier mâché to make many other objects – just use your imagination.

Getting Ready

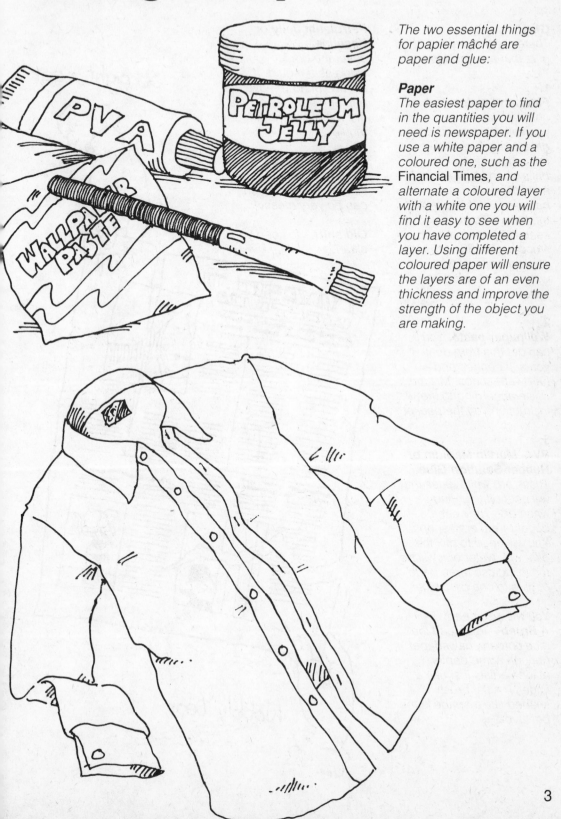

The two essential things for papier mâché are paper and glue:

Paper
The easiest paper to find in the quantities you will need is newspaper. If you use a white paper and a coloured one, such as the **Financial Times**, and alternate a coloured layer with a white one you will find it easy to see when you have completed a layer. Using different coloured paper will ensure the layers are of an even thickness and improve the strength of the object you are making.

Glue

There are three types of glue that are good to use:

1.
Flour and water. This is one you can make yourself. It's a good cheap glue, but will sometimes roll up into sticky little balls when brushed onto newspaper. If this happens you should pick the balls off carefully to keep the papier mâché smooth. Use 30g (1½ oz) of plain white flour mixed with 250cl (½ pint) of water.

2.
Wallpaper paste. You can get this from do-it-yourself centres and hardware shops. Mix the paste according to the instructions on the packet.

3.
PVA, Marvin Medium or Rubber Solution Glue. These are white glues that will peel off your fingers when dry. They can be bought from craft shops. You will need to mix the glue with water or it will be too thick: use three parts of glue to one part water.

You will also need:
A Brush – to spread the glue onto the newspaper (though some papier mâché artists just use a finger!). A flat brush shaped like a spade is the best type.

Petroleum Jelly or Vaseline – you use this to cover the object you are using as a mould. It allows you to remove the papier mâché when it is dry without damaging the mould.

Extra newspaper – to cover your working surface. Papier mâché can be very messy!

Old shirt – to keep you clean.

Straight tear

Wobbly tear

Preparing the newspaper

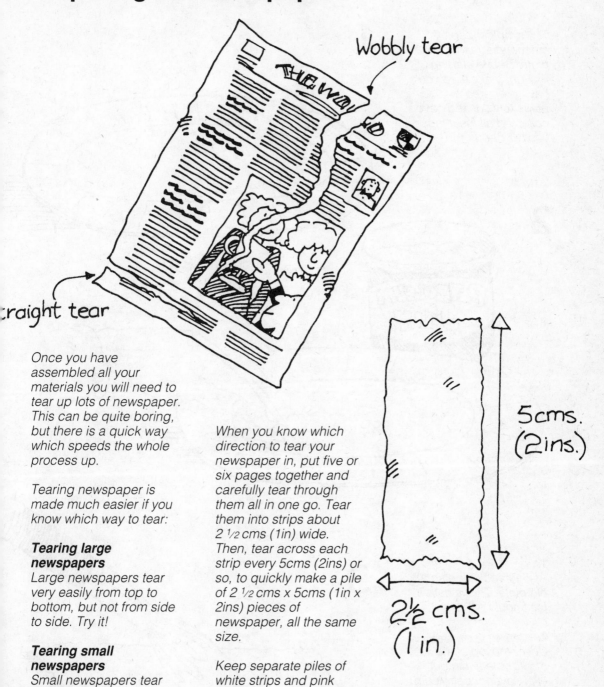

Wobbly tear

Straight tear

5cms. (2ins.)

2½ cms. (1 in.)

Once you have assembled all your materials you will need to tear up lots of newspaper. This can be quite boring, but there is a quick way which speeds the whole process up.

Tearing newspaper is made much easier if you know which way to tear:

Tearing large newspapers
Large newspapers tear very easily from top to bottom, but not from side to side. Try it!

Tearing small newspapers
Small newspapers tear differently. They tear very easily from side to side, but not from top to bottom. Try this too!

When you know which direction to tear your newspaper in, put five or six pages together and carefully tear through them all in one go. Tear them into strips about 2 ½ cms (1in) wide. Then, tear across each strip every 5cms (2ins) or so, to quickly make a pile of 2 ½ cms x 5cms (1in x 2ins) pieces of newspaper, all the same size.

Keep separate piles of white strips and pink ones.

You're now ready to start your first project.

Easy Mould Project

The simplest papier mâché shape to make is a plate. Before starting though, make sure you have prepared a good place to work and have collected all the things you will need.

1

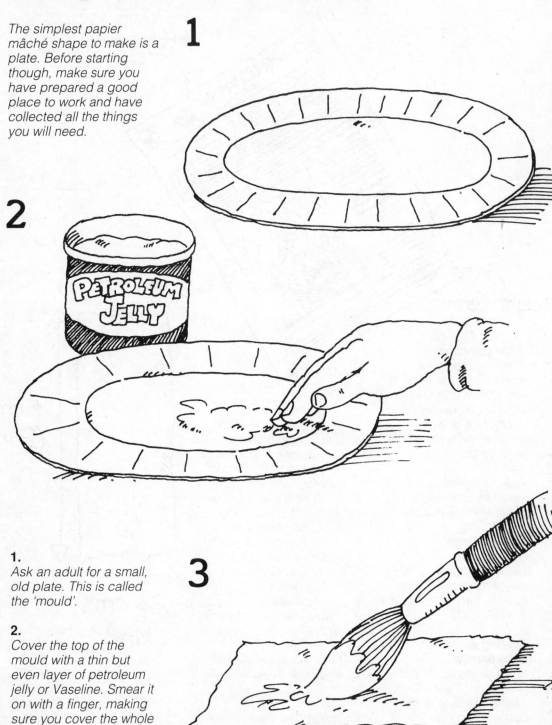

2

1.
Ask an adult for a small, old plate. This is called the 'mould'.

2.
Cover the top of the mould with a thin but even layer of petroleum jelly or Vaseline. Smear it on with a finger, making sure you cover the whole surface.

3

4

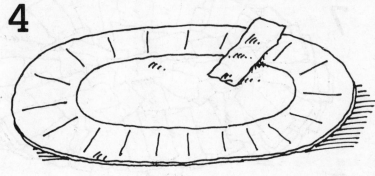

3.
Apply glue to a piece of white newspaper . . .

4.
. . . and put it on the mould so that it overlaps the edge, glue side up.

5.
Paste glue on to more pieces of newspaper, and stick them around the edge of the mould. Be careful not to leave any gaps between the pieces.

5

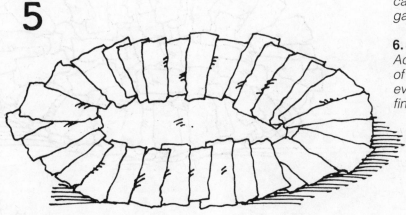

6.
Add pieces to the middle of the mould. Smooth everything flat with a finger as you go.

6

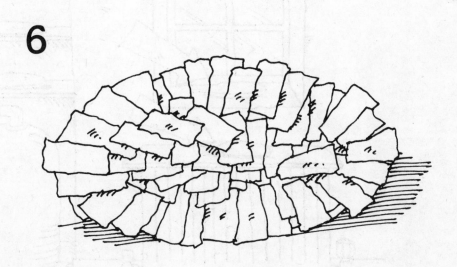

7.

When you have completely finished one layer, change newspaper colour and begin a second layer in exactly the same way as the first.

8.

Continue the process, making sure all the layers are flat and free of bumps as you go, until you have built up eight layers.

9.

Leaving the wet papier mâché on the mould, put it somewhere warm to dry. This could be on a sunny window-sill, on a shelf above a radiator or next to a boiler. Do not put it in the oven or under the grill. If you live somewhere hot you can leave it to dry out of doors. Be sure not to leave it where someone could sit or stand on it.

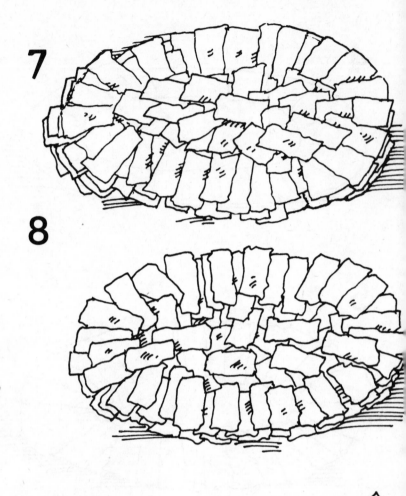

10

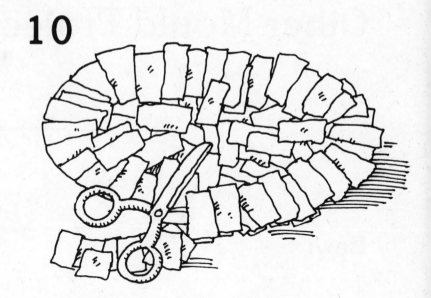

10..
After a day or so the papier mâché will be completely dry, and you can remove it from the mould. It should feel amazingly strong! Cut off the rough edge using a pair of strong safety scissors. You may need to ask an adult to help you with this.

11

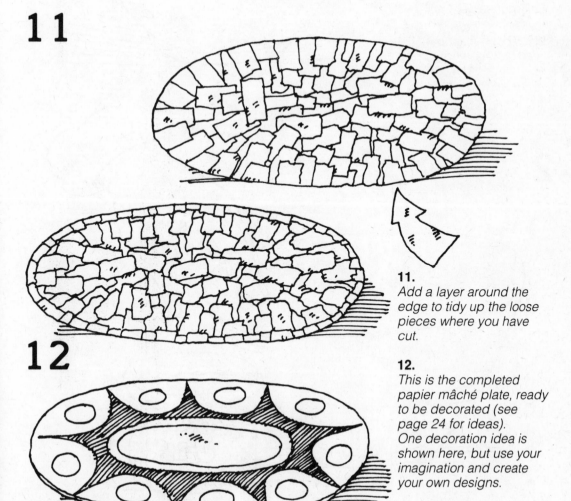

11.
Add a layer around the edge to tidy up the loose pieces where you have cut.

12

12.
This is the completed papier mâché plate, ready to be decorated (see page 24 for ideas). One decoration idea is shown here, but use your imagination and create your own designs.

Other Mould Projects

The papier mâché method shown on the previous pages will work with many other sorts of mould. Here are some ideas.

1

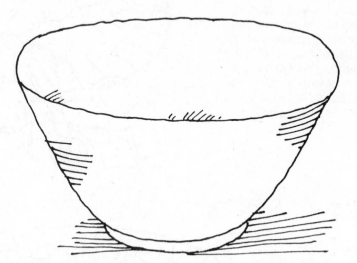

Bowl

1.
You can use any sort of bowl for this project: try a cereal bowl, fruit bowl, salad bowl or mixing bowl.

2

PETROLEUM JELLY

3

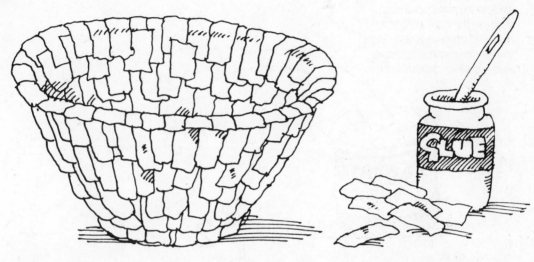

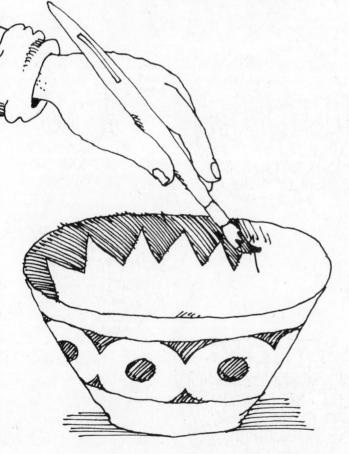

2.
Build up the papier mâché layers in just the same way as shown in the Easy Mould Project on page 6. Start by smearing petroleum jelly or Vaseline onto the inside (not the outside) of the dish, before applying the glued newspaper strips. Make about eight layers.

3.
This is the completed dish, ready to be decorated (see page 24 for ideas).

Bowl With Foot

The strips of newspaper should be torn up a little smaller for this project, or they will crease where they curve around the balloon. Aim for strips about 2cm x 4cm ($^3/_4$ x1 $^1/_2$ ins.).

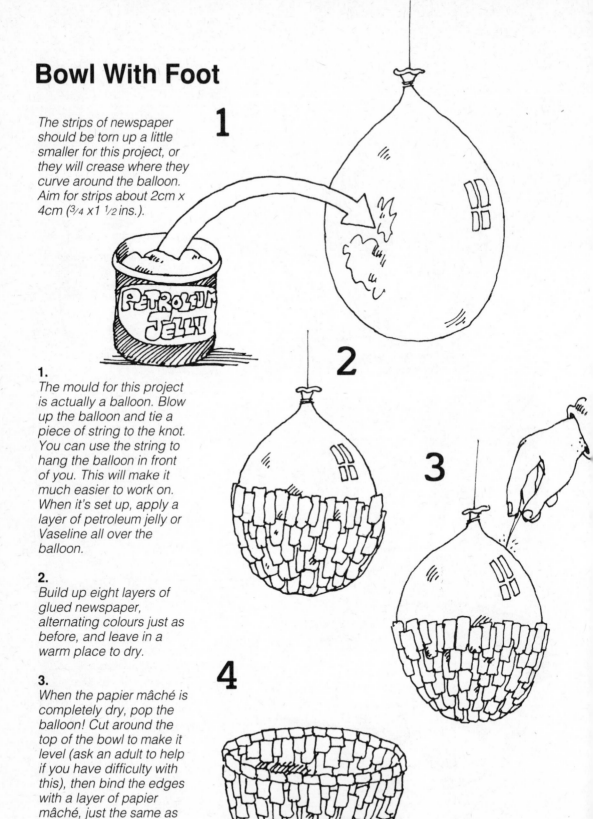

1.

The mould for this project is actually a balloon. Blow up the balloon and tie a piece of string to the knot. You can use the string to hang the balloon in front of you. This will make it much easier to work on. When it's set up, apply a layer of petroleum jelly or Vaseline all over the balloon.

2.

Build up eight layers of glued newspaper, alternating colours just as before, and leave in a warm place to dry.

3.

When the papier mâché is completely dry, pop the balloon! Cut around the top of the bowl to make it level (ask an adult to help if you have difficulty with this), then bind the edges with a layer of papier mâché, just the same as before.

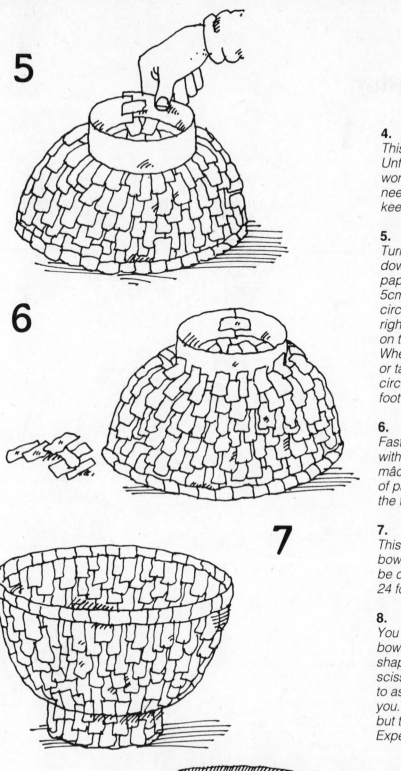

5

6

7

8

4.
This is the basic bowl. Unfortunately though . . . it won't stand up! You'll need to make a 'foot' to keep it standing up.

5.
Turn the bowl upside down. Roll a length of stiff paper or thin card about 5cms (2ins) wide into a circle, so that it looks the right shape when placed on the bottom of the bowl. When it looks good, glue or tape the ends of the circle together. This is the foot.

6.
Fasten the foot to the bowl with pieces of papier mâché. Apply two layers of papier mâché all over the foot, even the inside.

7.
This is the completed bowl with its foot, ready to be decorated (see page 24 for ideas).

8.
You can cut the finished bowl into interesting shapes using safety scissors – you may want to ask an adult to help you. Here are some ideas but there are many more. Experiment!

Bowl With Rim

1.
Make the papier mâché bowl exactly as described on page 10.

2.
Turn it upside-down onto a piece of card. Draw carefully around the rim.

3.
Remove the bowl, then draw another circle which is a little larger than the first.

1

2

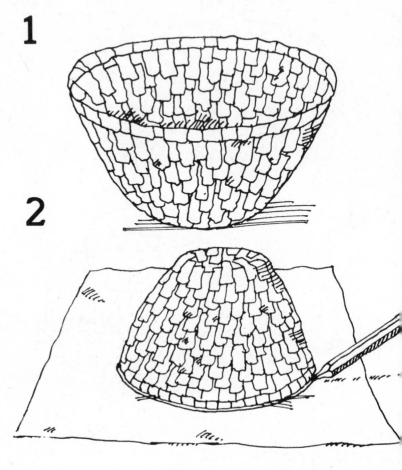

3

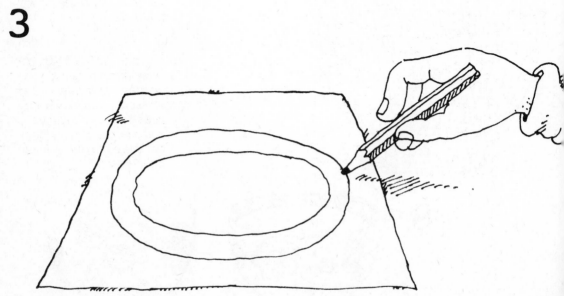

4

4.
Carefully cut out the ring of card between the two circles. Fasten it to the top of the papier mâché bowl using more pieces of newspaper. Cover the whole rim with two layers of papier mâché.

5.
This is the completed bowl with its rim, ready to be decorated (see page 24 for ideas).

6.
Experiment with the shape of the rim. It can have a wobbly edge, have holes cut in it, or even have handles. Copy one of these ideas or invent your own.

Make Your Own Moulds

So far in the book, all the papier mâché projects have been made using existing objects as moulds. However, it is also possible to make your own moulds. This is a lot of fun because you can make exactly what you want! The papier mâché method is just the same as before, so the only difference is in how to make the mould.

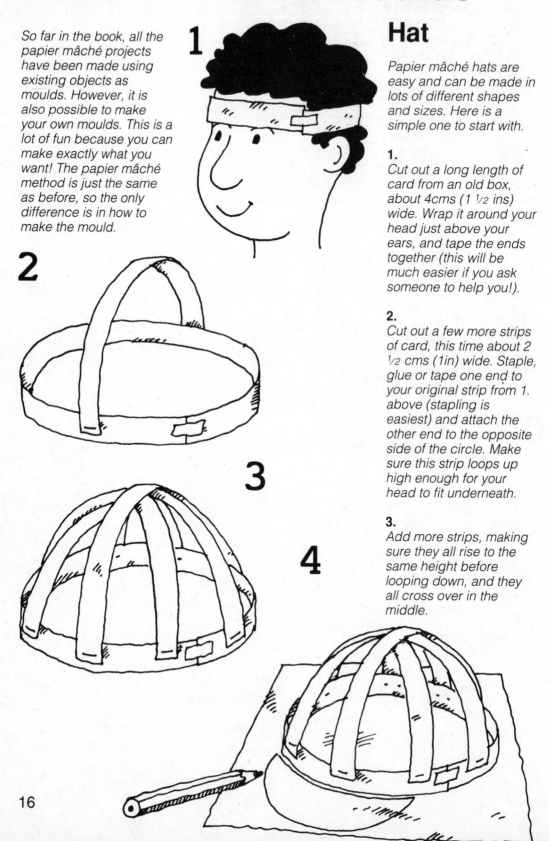

Hat

Papier mâché hats are easy and can be made in lots of different shapes and sizes. Here is a simple one to start with.

1.
Cut out a long length of card from an old box, about 4cms (1 ½ ins) wide. Wrap it around your head just above your ears, and tape the ends together (this will be much easier if you ask someone to help you!).

2.
Cut out a few more strips of card, this time about 2 ½ cms (1in) wide. Staple, glue or tape one end to your original strip from 1. above (stapling is easiest) and attach the other end to the opposite side of the circle. Make sure this strip loops up high enough for your head to fit underneath.

3.
Add more strips, making sure they all rise to the same height before looping down, and they all cross over in the middle.

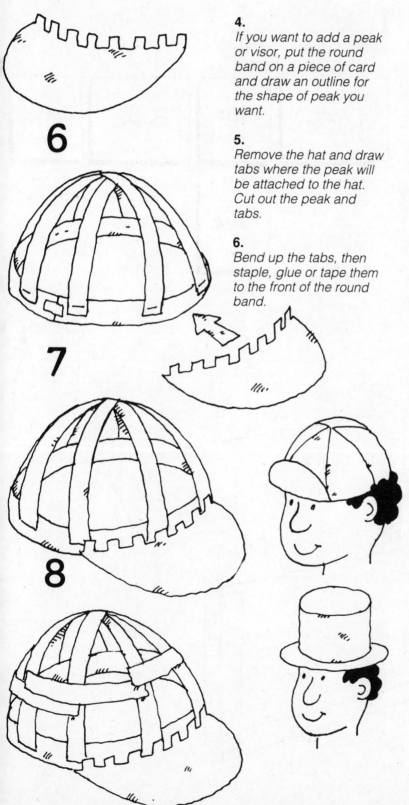

5

6

7

8

4.
If you want to add a peak or visor, put the round band on a piece of card and draw an outline for the shape of peak you want.

5.
Remove the hat and draw tabs where the peak will be attached to the hat. Cut out the peak and tabs.

6.
Bend up the tabs, then staple, glue or tape them to the front of the round band.

7.
This is the completed mould. It is now ready to be covered with papier mâché..

8.
Smear the mould with petroleum jelly or Vaseline, then apply strips of glued newspaper over the top. The method of applying the glued newspaper is exactly the same as before, though you may need to use slightly longer strips of newspaper to bridge the gaps on the mould. Build up eight layers, but **don't** put newspaper on the **underneath** of the peak, only on the top.

9.
When the papier mâché is dry, pull the mould out. The rim will be rough, so trim it with a pair of safety scissors, then bind over the rough edges with more newspaper, like the plate on page 6. Decorate it as you please, perhaps following one of the ideas on page 24, or the idea shown here.

The top hat is made in exactly the same way, but is even easier. Can you think how the mould was made? (Clue: the sides are a piece of rolled up card.)

Boxes

Papier mâché boxes can be made in any shape or size, with or without a lid. They are **very strong** and have hundreds of uses.

1.
Decide how big you want your box to be. Carefully draw the outline on a piece of card. Don't worry about making the lid now; if you want to put one on it is best to do it later.

2.
Cut out the outline on the card and tape the edges together to make the box shape.

1

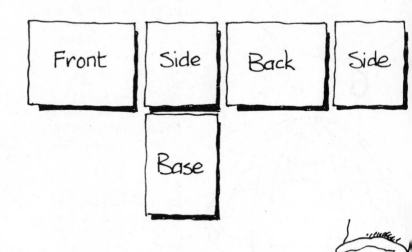

2

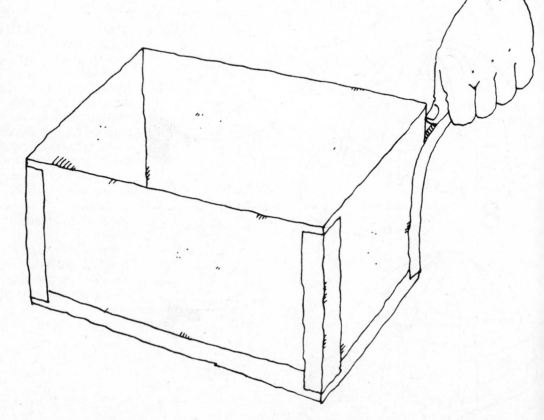

3

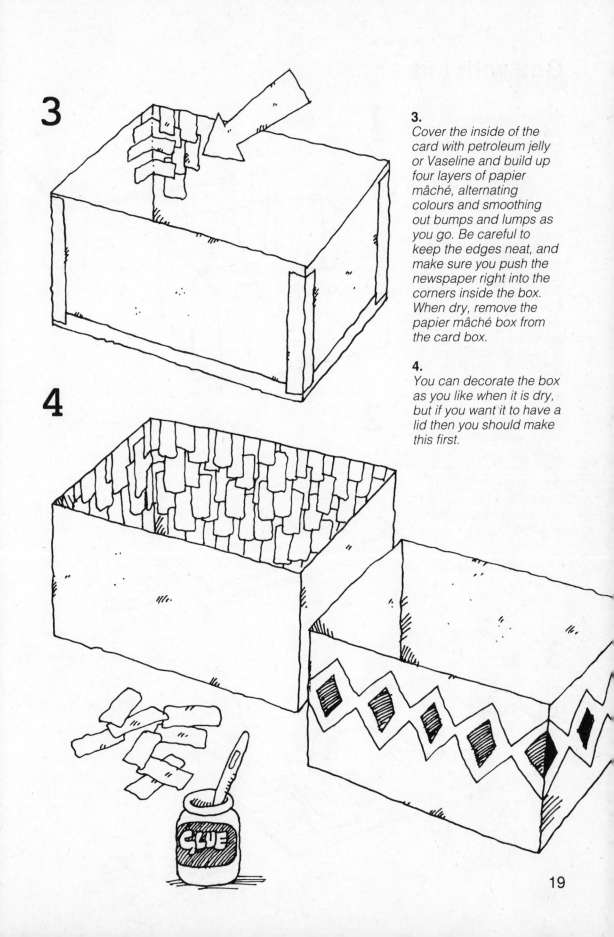

3.

Cover the inside of the card with petroleum jelly or Vaseline and build up four layers of papier mâché, alternating colours and smoothing out bumps and lumps as you go. Be careful to keep the edges neat, and make sure you push the newspaper right into the corners inside the box. When dry, remove the papier mâché box from the card box.

4.

You can decorate the box as you like when it is dry, but if you want it to have a lid then you should make this first.

4

Box with Lid

Before making the lid, make the complete papier mâché box as described above.

1.
For the lid, cut out a piece of brown corrugated card from an old box, so that it loosely fits inside the top of the papier mâché box. This is piece 'A'.

2.
Glue piece 'A' to a slightly larger piece of card. This is piece 'B'. Turn it upside-down.

3.
To make a handle, tape a short length of string or ribbon to the top of the lid. Then cover the whole lid (top and bottom) with four layers of papier mâché, being careful to keep it neat where the handle joins the lid.

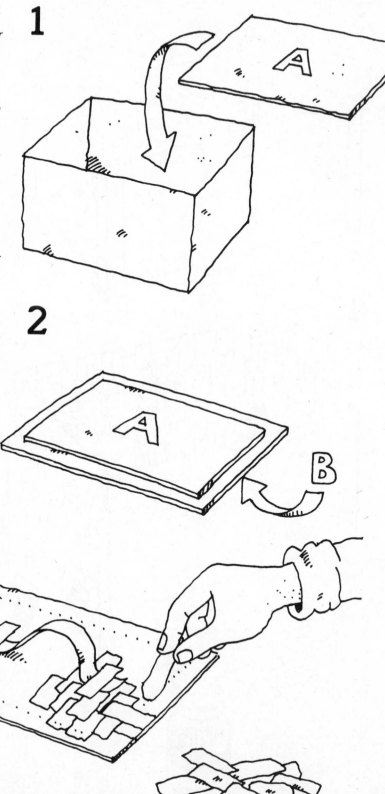

4

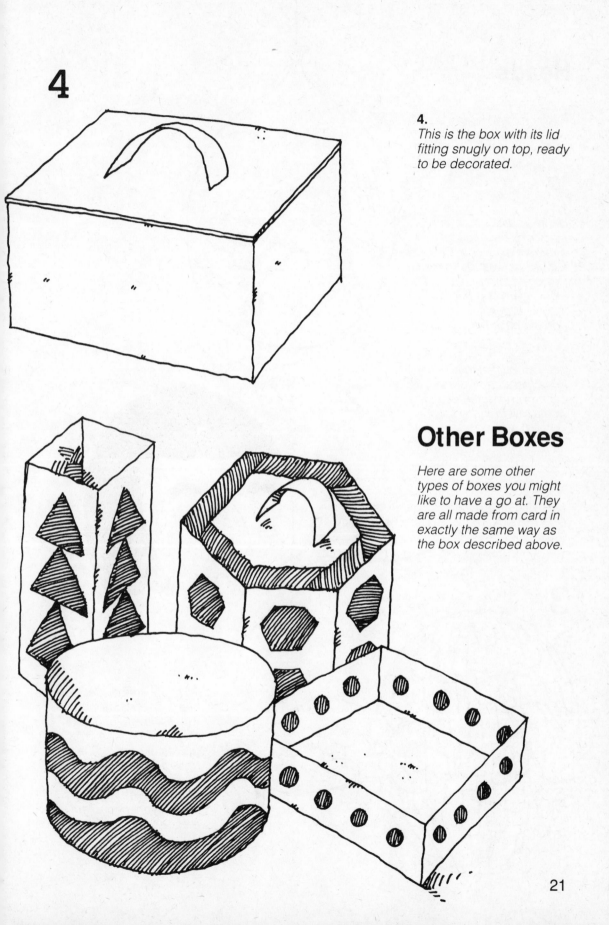

4.
This is the box with its lid fitting snugly on top, ready to be decorated.

Other Boxes

Here are some other types of boxes you might like to have a go at. They are all made from card in exactly same way as the box described above.

Heads

Papier mâché heads are easily made using balloons as moulds. This is how you make a simple head:

1.
Hang a balloon from a piece of string, so that you can work all over it. Cover the balloon with petroleum jelly or Vaseline, then eight layers of papier mâché. When it is dry . . . pop the balloon!

2.
You can paint it to look like a friend, a favourite cartoon character, or just with a silly or funny face.

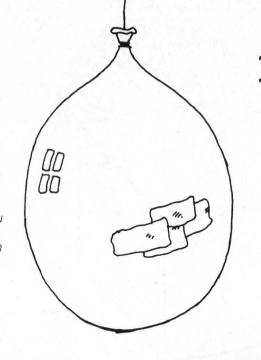

1

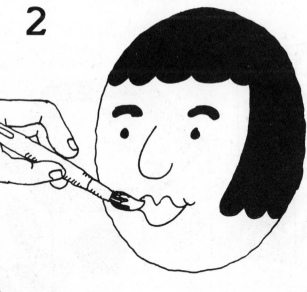

2

3

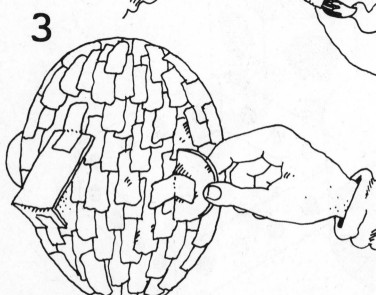

3.
To make a more detailed head, cover a balloon with six layers of papier mâché, then tape on pieces of card for the nose and ears. Cover these pieces and the rest of the balloon with two more layers of papier mâché.

4

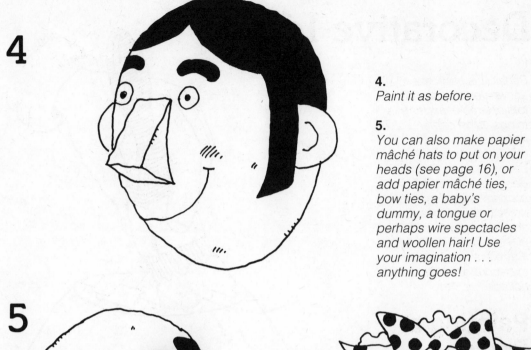

4.
Paint it as before.

5.
You can also make papier mâché hats to put on your heads (see page 16), or add papier mâché ties, bow ties, a baby's dummy, a tongue or perhaps wire spectacles and woollen hair! Use your imagination . . . anything goes!

5

Decorative Ideas

So far, this book has shown you how to make lots of simple, exciting things using papier mâché, but it hasn't shown you how to decorate them. Properly decorated, even the simplest papier mâché object will look beautiful and impressive.

There are two main ways to decorate: painting and collage.

Painting a Design

Before painting a design onto dry papier mâché you will need to prime it. Priming means painting one or two layers of clean white emulsion paint all over your papier mâché object (you can use coloured emulsion if you prefer). This does two important things. Firstly, it gives a clean surface to paint on, and secondly, it stops the paint from soaking right into all the papier mâché layers when you decorate your object. This makes decorating quicker and you'll use less paint. Half-empty tins of emulsion can be found in most houses, so ask an adult to find one for you.

Use poster paints or powder paints to paint your design. If you know how to use them, watercolour, acrylic and oil paints are also OK to use. The paint can be put on thickly, or watered down first. It may help to draw the outline of your design onto the primed surface, before beginning to paint. You should experiment with your designs. If something doesn't work out, simply wait for it to dry and paint over it!

Felt Pens

Prime the papier mâché as described above, then colour the surface with felt pens. Pens with a wide nib can cover large areas very quickly, whereas ordinary felt pens are ideal for detail.

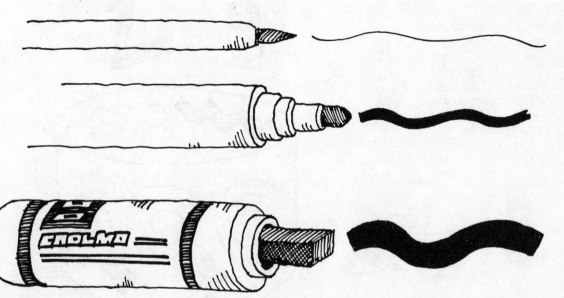

Collage

A papier mâché object that has been decorated with paint or felt pens loses its 'papery' look. If you want to keep the papery look you can use collage to decorate your objects.

1.

The bowl shown here was first covered with a layer of pale pieces of paper cut from magazine photographs. Then black paper squares were stuck over the top to create a pattern. This mosaic is easy to do but gives a very professional finish.

2.

Another way to create a collage pattern is to cut out shapes from sheets of coloured paper bought in a shop, or from sheets you have coloured yourself with paints or felt pens. These cut-out shapes can be glued onto the primed surface, or onto a paper mosaic surface (as described in 1. above). Cutting out painted shapes and sticking them to your object is often easier and quicker than painting them on.

1

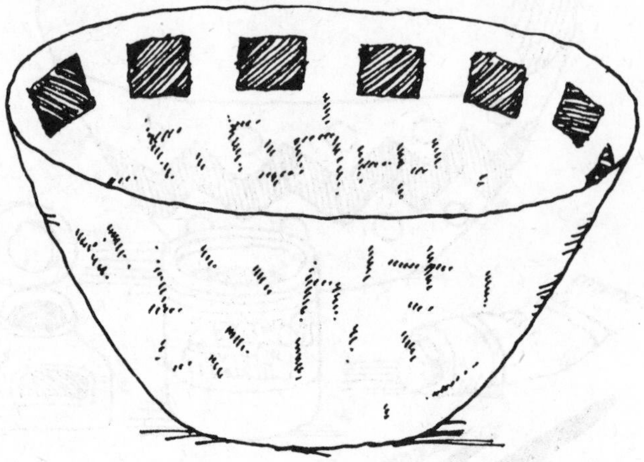

2

Protecting Papier Mâché

It is important to protect your papier mâché objects immediately after you have decorated them, or they will soon become damaged. The best way to protect the surface is to cover it with varnish.

Varnish is the perfect way to protect papier mâché. It is made with oil, so it will protect a painted or collaged surface from water and steam, making it completely waterproof.

You won't need to use much varnish, and most houses will have half-empty tins of it lying around. If you can't find any, ask a friend or neighbour, or you can buy it at do-it-yourself centres and hardware shops. The best varnish to use for protecting papier mâché objects is clear varnish.

You must ask an adult to help you use varnish because it can be very difficult to clear up if spilled or dripped in the wrong place, or if it gets onto your skin. Use it very carefully!

Put two thin coats onto your papier mâché object, allowing the first coat to dry for a day before applying the second coat. Varnish will not only protect the surface from damage, but it will strengthen what you have made and also give it a shiny, professional finish.

Papier Mâché Presents

Papier mâché presents are fun, easy and cheap to make, and they're much nicer to receive than presents bought at a shop. You can make them for your family and friends, or just for yourself as a treat! You can really go to town decorating them.

Useful Bowls and Boxes

Fruit Bowl
Follow the instructions on page 10 using a large kitchen mixing bowl for the mould. Decorate your bowl and varnish it for a really professional finish.

Plant Pot
Use a plastic plant pot for the mould, and put the papier mâché layers on the **inside** of the pot. Follow the instructions for the bowl you made earlier (page 10). When you have decorated it, give it three or four thin coats of varnish to make it completely waterproof.

Jewellery Box
You can make the jewellery box with or without a lid. Start by making your own mould from card, then follow the instructions on page 18.

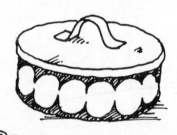

Beautiful Ornamental Bowl
Ornamental bowls make excellent presents and look wonderful on a table or shelf. Give the bowl a foot (see page 12) and a rim (see page 14). Decorate it very carefully.

Pen Holder
Make your own mould from card (see page 18), either as a flat box, or as an upright box. Be careful to make your box the right size to hold all the pens you need.

Waste Paper Basket
Use an existing metal waste paper basket as the mould and make it like the bowl (see page 10). Alternatively you could make you own mould using strips of card, as though making a hat (see page 16).

Cassette or Video Box
Make a mould from strong card, then cover it with papier mâché (see page 18). Be careful to measure your mould carefully so that the video and audio tapes will fit in when it's finished.

Desk Tidy
This is a flat box made like the pen holder above, but divided into compartments with pieces of card. Make a plain box mould from card, following the instructions on page 18. Then cut out strips of card and tape or staple them in place inside the box, dividing it up into sections. Make a list of all the things people have in their desks, like paper clips, elastic bands, drawing pins, crayons etc., and make enough compartments to store them all.

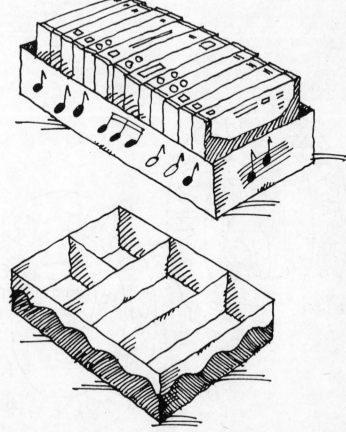

Wall Plaques

These are papier mâché plaques, made using simple plate moulds, as shown on page 6. They are fastened to the wall for display, using a wire support.

1.
Plaques can be made for a special birthday, such as an eighteenth or twenty-first, and given instead of a card. Or they can be given to a team who have won a competition, to someone moving away or passing exams, as a special Valentine's Day card, to someone coming out of hospital, for Mother's Day or Father's Day . . . and for many, many other occasions.

2.
To make the wire support, use an old coat hanger or wire from a florist's shop. You will need an adult to help you cut it to length. Cut a piece a bit longer than the width of your plaque and bend it in the middle. Bend the ends of the wire over the rim of the plaque to support it. The bend in the middle of the wire hooks over a small nail, screw or picture hook placed in the wall.

Think about how you will decorate or write on your plaque. You might find it useful to try out your designs on rough paper until they are just as you want them. You should varnish the plaque so that it won't become damaged.

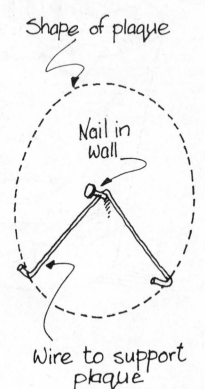

Shape of plaque

Nail in wall

Wire to support plaque

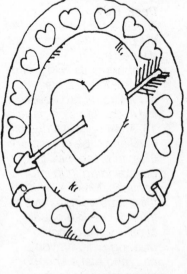

Jewellery

Papier mâché jewellery is very fashionable and many people make and sell it. Not only does it look good, but it's cheap and easy to make so you can build up a huge jewellery collection.

Remember to varnish what you make and ask an adult to help you put clasps onto earrings and safety pins onto brooches.

Finger Rings
Cut a small strip of thin card and loop it around your finger so that it is a loose fit. Glue the ends together. Wrap a few layers of small pieces of papier mâché around the card. These layers will stiffen the ring (when dry, not when wet) and tighten the loose ring on the finger. Crumpled-up balls of papier mâché make excellent stones for rings. Decorate the ring with gold or silver paint, then varnish it.

Earrings
First decide what shape you want your earrings to be, then draw it on a piece of card and cut it out carefully. Then draw round it on another piece of card and cut this out too. You will now have two identical pieces of card with which to make a matching pair of earrings.

Cover the card shape with a few layers of papier mâché. When the papier mâché is dry ask an adult to help you attach proper earring clasps (they can be bought very cheaply at markets). Use your imagination when decorating your earrings. You could even use fluorescent paint and glitter.

Bangles
Bangles are made in the same way as finger rings, but you should wrap the strip of card loosely round your wrist to make a mould of the right size.

Brooches
Brooches are made following the instructions for earrings. Experiment with the size of the brooches you make. Ask an adult to help you fasten a safety pin to the back of the brooch, so that you can pin it onto your clothes.

*Lions is an imprint of
HarperCollins Children's Books,
a division of HarperCollins
Publishers Ltd, 77-85 Fulham
Palace Road, Hammersmith,
London W6 8JB*

ISBN: 0 00 196395-3

*Designed and Typeset
by: axis design
Set in Helvetica Light Italic 10/11
Printed and bound in Hong Kong*